W9-AEY-813

DISCARD

JUL 2005

— Discovering Canada —

Samuel de Champlain

Heather C. Hudak

Weigl
CALGARY
www.weigl.ca

Published by Weigl Educational Publishers Limited
6325 – 10 Street SE
Calgary, Alberta, Canada
T2H 2Z9

Web site: www.weigl.ca

Library and Archives Canada Cataloguing in Publication
Hudak, Heather C., 1975-
    Samuel de Champlain / Heather C. Hudak.
(Discovering Canada)
Includes index.
ISBN 1-55388-064-1 (bound).--ISBN 1-55388-117-6 (pbk.)
    1. Champlain, Samuel de, 1567-1635--Juvenile literature.
2. Canada--Discovery and exploration--French--Juvenile literature.
3. Explorers--France--Biography--Juvenile literature. 4. Explorers--Canada--
Biography--Juvenile literature. I. Title. II. Series: Discovering Canada (Calgary,
Alta.)

FC332.H83 2004   j971.01'13'092   C2004-904876-7

Printed in the United States of America
1 2 3 4 5 6 7 8 9 0   08 07 06 05 04

We acknowledge the
financial support of the
Government of Canada
through the Book
Publishing Industry
Development Program
(BPIDP) for our
publishing activities.

**PROJECT
COORDINATOR**
Janice L. Redlin

COPY EDITOR
Tina Schwartzenberger

DESIGN
Terry Paulhus

LAYOUT
Terry Paulhus

PHOTO RESEARCHER
Ken Price

On the Cover
Samuel de Champlain
was known as the Father
of New France.

CREDITS: Every reasonable effort
has been made to trace ownership
and to obtain permission to reprint
copyright material. The publishers
would be pleased to have any
errors or omissions brought to their
attention so that they may be
corrected in subsequent printings.

Cover: Clipart.com (Samuel de Champlain); **Warren Clark:** pages 17, 19, 21, 26-27; **Clipart.com:**
pages 5, 6, 26TL, 26TR, 26BL, 26BR, 30; **Comstock.com:** pages 1, 10; **Corel Corporation:** page 11;
Heather C. Hudak: page 29B; **The Mariners' Museum:** page 13; **Maryevans.com:** page 7;
National Archives of Canada: pages 20, 22, 23, 24; **Northwindpictures.com:** page 18;
Photos.com: pages 3, 8, 9, 12, 14T, 14B, 15, 16, 29T; **Courtesy of Rogers Communications Inc.:**
page 4; **Lee Snider:** page 25.

CONTENTS

Introduction

ailing across the vast Atlantic Ocean, Samuel de Champlain charted the land now known as Canada. He braved bitterly cold winters and deadly diseases in the process. Champlain was the first person to accurately map the land. He was also the first European to build a successful settlement in Canada. Champlain established friendly trade relationships with some Native Peoples, but he fought with others. Between 1608 and 1638, Champlain explored new routes, charted unknown territory, and observed life in Canada. The Father of New France, as Champlain became known, made his mark on the New World.

■ Samuel de Champlain was sent to New France to establish a trading post and protect France's control over the fur trade industry.

Curiosity about wealth and need for simplified trade routes drove European explorers to sail across the ocean.

985 The Vikings first visited Canada's northeastern regions.

1000 Viking Leif "the Lucky" Ericson reached Canada. He settled in Vinland, which may be the area now known as L'Anse aux Meadows in Newfoundland and Labrador. Archaeologists found Viking artifacts in this area in the 1960s.

Those who explored Canada, such as Champlain, covered a large territory. They battled difficult weather conditions to chart Canada's land. From the Atlantic to the Pacific and Arctic Oceans, and across the land between, there was much to discover. Although Champlain was not the first explorer to reach the soil of New France, as Canada was called at this time, he was one of the most important. Champlain spent many hours recording his experiences.

■ A steering wheel is connected to a rudder located at the rear end of a boat. The rudder is a flat piece of wood or metal that can be turned side to side in the water, controlling the direction a boat travels.

1497 John Cabot sailed to Newfoundland and Labrador in search of the Far East.

1534 Jacques Cartier first sailed to Canada in search of new lands to claim for the king of France.

1603 Samuel de Champlain sailed to Canada. He was the first person to accurately map the land.

1609 Henry Hudson sailed to what is now Newfoundland and Labrador. Then he travelled south and discovered the Hudson River.

Early Years

Very little is known about Champlain's early years. For example, the exact date of Champlain's birth is unknown. He was born around 1567 in a small seaport town called Brouage, in the province of Saintonge in France. It was an important harbour for the salt trade, and many boats sailed to Newfoundland and Labrador from this place.

Champlain's father's was a naval captain named Antoine Champlain. His mother was Marguerite Le Roy. Champlain sailed with his father many times. During these trips, Champlain became a skilled **navigator**. A local priest educated him when he was not sailing. Champlain also served as a **quartermaster** in the French army during the Wars of Religion.

Explorer Essentials

In 1598, King Henry IV created the Edict of Nantes. The edict established rights for French Protestants, allowing them to practise their religion within specific guidelines and offering people who practise this faith **civil rights**. The edict ended the Wars of Religion.

■ There are no authentic portraits of Champlain. However, this illustration presents him as Morris Bishop, in 1948, described Champlain—"a lean, ascetic type, dry, dark, probably rather under than over normal size; fully bearded; dark hair and eyes."

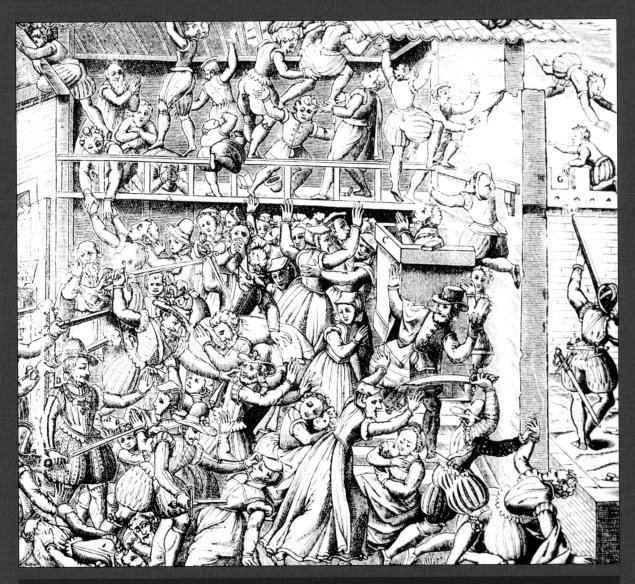

WARS OF RELIGION

Between 1562 and 1598, the French Catholics and the Huguenots, or French Protestants, fought against each other in a series of civil wars. French Protestants wanted the right to freely practise their religion. At the same time, three families of nobility struggled to maintain power and control of the crown.

One family sided with the Huguenots, another family sided with the Catholics, and the third family divided their support between the two religions. After several wars and bloody **massacres**, Spain was called to aid the Catholics in their rebellion against French King Henry IV. The king wished to grant the Protestants freedom of religion.

Champlain's Ventures

Unemployed after the wars, Champlain returned to the sea. He sailed with his uncle, Guillaume Allene, the king of Spain's chief pilot. Champlain accompanied his uncle to Spain. He sailed on a ship returning Spanish soldiers to their homeland after serving in France during the war.

In 1599, Champlain took to the waters as captain of one of his uncle's ships, the *St. Julien*. Champlain and his crew sailed toward the West Indies, stopping in Guadeloupe, Vera Cruz, Puerto Rico, and Mexico. For more than 2 years, he explored the area, recording his observations and charting the land. Champlain sailed through Panama before returning to Spain in 1601. In 1601, his uncle gave him a large property near LaRochelle. Champlain also received a small pension for his service as a geographer to King Henry IV.

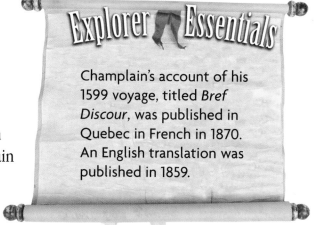

Explorer Essentials

Champlain's account of his 1599 voyage, titled *Bref Discour*, was published in Quebec in French in 1870. An English translation was published in 1859.

■ The Gulf of Mexico is an arm of the Atlantic Ocean. Champlain kept a detailed journal about his expedition to this area.

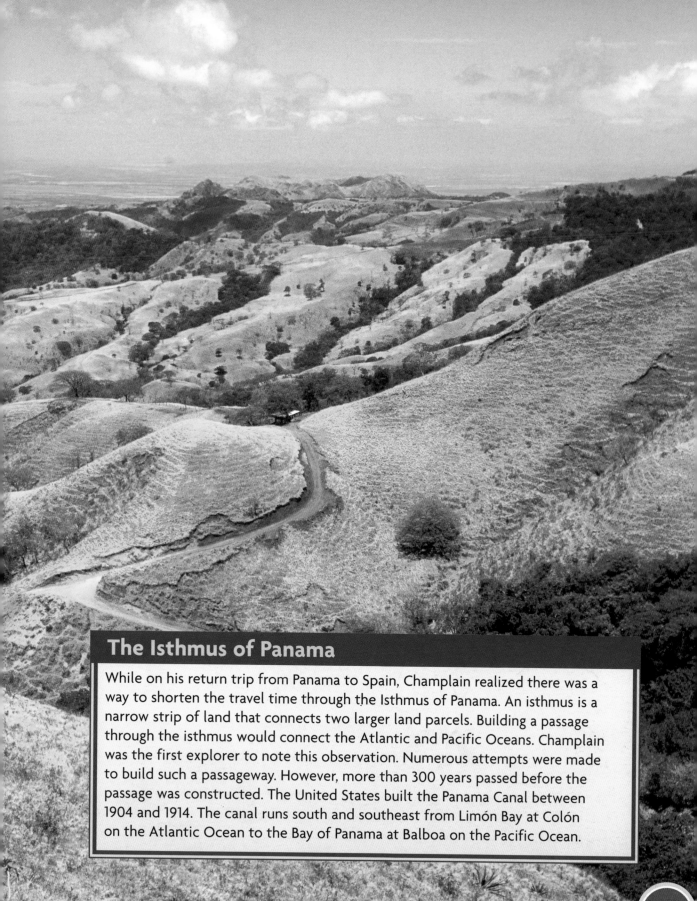

The Isthmus of Panama

While on his return trip from Panama to Spain, Champlain realized there was a way to shorten the travel time through the Isthmus of Panama. An isthmus is a narrow strip of land that connects two larger land parcels. Building a passage through the isthmus would connect the Atlantic and Pacific Oceans. Champlain was the first explorer to note this observation. Numerous attempts were made to build such a passageway. However, more than 300 years passed before the passage was constructed. The United States built the Panama Canal between 1904 and 1914. The canal runs south and southeast from Limón Bay at Colón on the Atlantic Ocean to the Bay of Panama at Balboa on the Pacific Ocean.

Exploring for Riches

Throughout the late 1500s, many European countries had successfully established trade relationships with the Native Peoples of New France. New France had an abundance of furs, cod, and whale oil, which Europeans wanted to acquire. After the Wars of Religion ended, France grew interested in similar trade opportunities.

Explorers required funding to sail across the ocean to New France. The king of France had once funded such ventures. Then, companies began to provide funds to send explorers overseas. In return, the king offered companies **monopolies** over **colonial** trade. This meant that companies funding voyages had exclusive control over selling and producing goods.

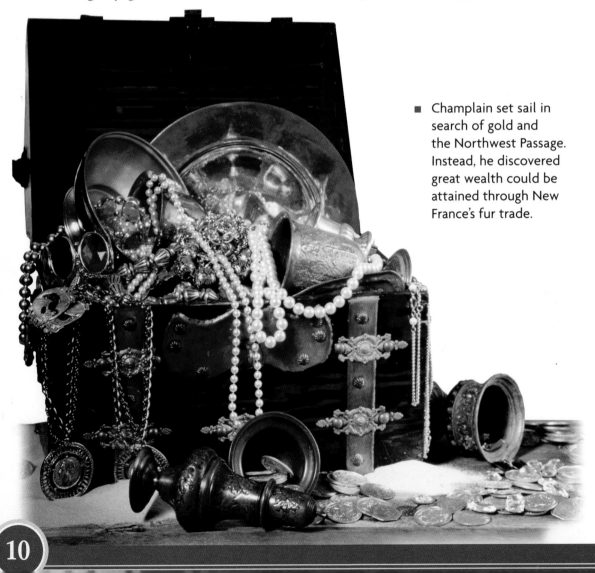

- Champlain set sail in search of gold and the Northwest Passage. Instead, he discovered great wealth could be attained through New France's fur trade.

Champlain, a skilled navigator and **cartographer**, quickly found work in France. Aymer de Chaste, the governor of Dieppe, had an interest in Champlain's early explorations. De Chaste wanted to learn more about trade opportunities in New France. He was looking for a crew to head an expedition. After securing money from the king of France and several **merchants**, de Chaste approached Champlain about taking part in a trade mission. De Chaste hired Gravé du Pont, a merchant with fur trade experience, to lead the expedition. On March 15, 1603, Champlain sailed on his first voyage between France and New France.

Explorer Essentials

Between 1534 and 1763, France controlled several colonies in North America. This area, which became known as New France, included the shores along the St. Lawrence River, what is now Newfoundland and Labrador, Acadia, and the Great Lakes region. Acadia is the area now known as Nova Scotia, New Brunswick, and Prince Edward Island.

Fur Trade Fortune

European men and women enjoyed wearing fur garments. Many people desired beaver fur for hats and clothes because it was warm and attractive.

The beaver was nearly extinct in Europe, so traders came to New France to obtain pelts. Beaver pelts had a soft underfur that, when made into felt, was warmer and more durable than woven materials. Long guard hairs protected the beaver's soft underfur. Europeans combed the pelts to remove these hairs. Whenever possible, they preferred to acquire pelts from Native Peoples. The Native Peoples would wear the pelts so that the guard hairs would rub off. Then, the Europeans did not have to comb the pelts.

Ships and Tools

Between 1603 and 1635, Champlain travelled to New France twelve times. Historians believe he travelled across the Atlantic Ocean in galleons. Galleons were large sailing ships that were often used to sail on long ocean journeys in the 1500s to 1700s. Galleons had a wooden galley and three or more **masts**. These ships were used for trade missions or war.

Most early explorers, such as Champlain, travelled with large crews. Often, many crewmembers aboard ships did not have much experience at sea. Many crewmembers became ill or died. Captains had to replace lost crewmembers. The crew worked the sails and **rigging**. They also made repairs and cared for the ship while at sea. Most ships also had a pilot or first mate. This person was responsible for navigating the ship. Other crewmembers included the cook, who was usually an injured crewmember who could not perform another duty, a **parson**, a surgeon, a carpenter, and a **boatswain**.

■ Galleons were the main sailing ships of the sixteenth and seventeenth centuries. They travelled fast even when carrying a large cargo.

Explorer Essentials

Thirty-five astrolabes belonging to Champlain have survived since the 1600s. One that was discovered in 1867 is in the care of the Canadian Museum of Civilization.

Champlain explored New France in a birchbark canoe. He watched the Native Peoples carry the lightweight canoes easily over rough waters. The canoes could carry a single passenger or as many as fifty people, as well as a large cargo of furs. The canoes were 3 to 7 metres long.

Some of the tools Champlain used to navigate the seas and chart the land included a **mariner**'s astrolabe and a compass. Astrolabes are used to show the position of objects in the sky at an exact place and time. A mariner's astrolabe determined the **latitude** of a ship. Champlain used a magnetic compass to determine direction. His compass had a magnetic needle pointing in the direction of the magnetic North Pole, as influenced by Earth's **magnetic field**.

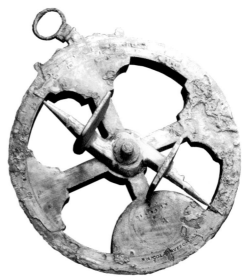

■ Champlain portaged and climbed over fallen logs near Green Lake, now also known as Astrolabe Lake. Many nineteenth-century authors believe Champlain lost his astrolabe at this location.

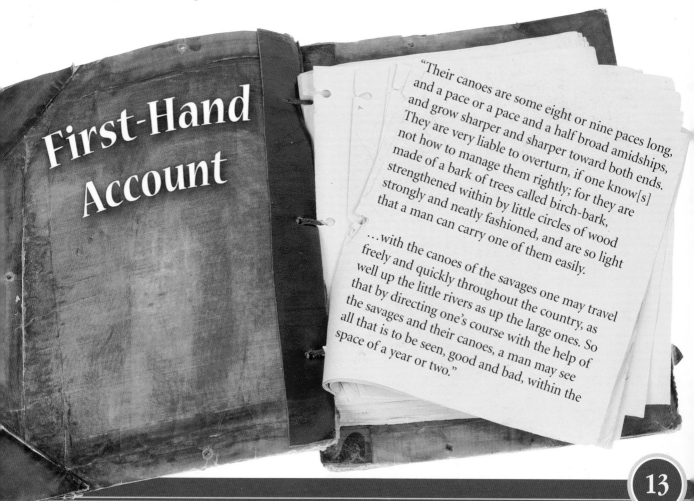

First-Hand Account

"Their canoes are some eight or nine paces long, and a pace or a pace and a half broad amidships, and grow sharper and sharper toward both ends. They are very liable to overturn, if one know[s] not how to manage them rightly; for they are made of a bark of trees called birch-bark, strengthened within by little circles of wood strongly and neatly fashioned, and are so light that a man can carry one of them easily.

…with the canoes of the savages one may travel freely and quickly throughout the country, as well up the little rivers as up the large ones. So that by directing one's course with the help of the savages and their canoes, a man may see all that is to be seen, good and bad, within the space of a year or two."

Sailing Supplies

It was difficult to store food and supplies on ships. Large amounts of water poured from the ocean into ships. Crews were at sea for long periods of time. Ships also lacked proper **ventilation**. Rats and insects infested food supplies. Sometimes, food suppliers sent spoiled food. Storing water proved another problem aboard ships. Fresh water often spoiled in barrels. Crewmembers sought fresh water on dry land.

Crews packed ships with sea biscuits and salted or dried beef or pork. Sea biscuits, or hardtack, were made from flour and water. They were cooked twice so they would stay dry at sea. Crewmembers dunked the biscuits in water to soften them. They were often filled with maggots or **weevils**.

Explorer Essentials

In the mid-1700s, British naval surgeon James Lind discovered that drinking lime, lemon, or orange juice could prevent scurvy.

■ Maggots are the legless, worm-like larvae of flies.

- Weevils are large beetles with downward-turning snouts. They cause damage to fruit, nuts, stems, and roots.

Crews also packed cheese, onions, dried beans, oatmeal, butter, sugar, peas, and salted or fresh fish. It was not possible to carry fresh fruit and vegetables aboard ships. These items, which contained vitamin C, spoiled quickly. As a result, crewmembers often suffered from scurvy, an illness caused by a lack of vitamin C. Scurvy caused the skin and gums to rot and teeth to fall out.

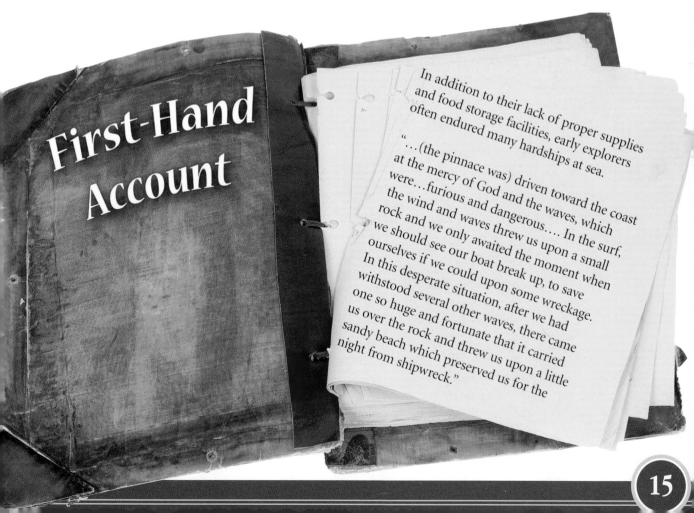

First-Hand Account

In addition to their lack of proper supplies and food storage facilities, early explorers often endured many hardships at sea.

"…(the pinnace was) driven toward the coast at the mercy of God and the waves, which were…furious and dangerous…. In the surf, the wind and waves threw us upon a small rock and we only awaited the moment when we should see our boat break up, to save ourselves if we could upon some wreckage. In this desperate situation, after we had withstood several other waves, there came one so huge and fortunate that it carried us over the rock and threw us upon a little sandy beach which preserved us for the night from shipwreck."

15

Across the Atlantic

hamplain's first voyage across the Atlantic was with Gravé du Pont in 1603. In New France, the crew docked at Tadoussac. They sailed up the St. Lawrence River and the Saguenay River until they reached the St. Louis rapids near Montreal. Champlain also sailed up to Gaspé, which he believed was a route to Asia. The crew returned to France later that year. Champlain published a report of his voyage titled *Des sauvages*.

Champlain returned to New France in 1604 on an expedition with the lieutenant general of Acadia, Pierre du Gua de Monts. The crew sought locations to establish a **colony** along the east coast of Acadia. First, they settled on an island in the St. Croix River.

Today, this area is the border between New Brunswick and Maine. After spending a long, harsh winter in St. Croix, the crew relocated to Port Royal, which is now known as Annapolis, Nova Scotia. During his visit, which lasted 3 years, Champlain charted the Bay of Fundy, the Annapolis Valley, and the Atlantic coast between the Saint John River and Cape Cod.

The French king's desire to build a settlement along the St. Lawrence funded Champlain's third expedition. In 1608, he commanded one of two ships sent to colonize New France. While the other ship traded for furs with Native Peoples to pay for the

■ In 1604, Champlain and Pierre du Gua de Monts explored the Bay of Fundy area before choosing to settle on an island at the mouth of the St. Croix River.

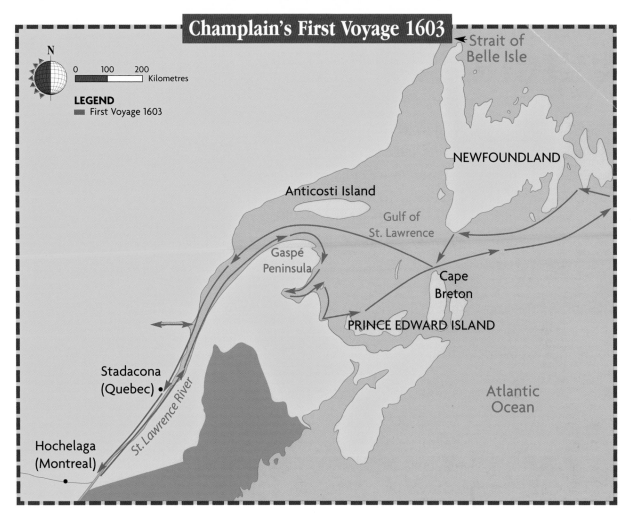

Champlain's First Voyage 1603

LEGEND

■ First Voyage 1603

0 100 200 Kilometres

N

Strait of Belle Isle

NEWFOUNDLAND

Anticosti Island

Gulf of St. Lawrence

Gaspé Peninsula

Cape Breton

PRINCE EDWARD ISLAND

Stadacona (Quebec)

St. Lawrence River

Atlantic Ocean

Hochelaga (Montreal)

expedition, Champlain explored and established a settlement and fur trade centre. In July, Champlain founded Quebec, the first permanent European colony in New France. Twenty-five settlers travelled with Champlain, but only nine survived the winter. More settlers arrived the following summer. In 1609, Champlain fought with the Huron, Algonquin, and Montagnais in wars against the Iroquois. Champlain also discovered the lake that now bears his name before returning to France for supplies.

Explorer Essentials

In 1609, as Champlain navigated south along New York waters, British explorer Henry Hudson moved north along the same path. Although the two never crossed paths, they encountered similar sites, cultures, and events.

Extended Exploration

Champlain travelled to New France for a short stay in 1610. In a fight with the Iroquois, an arrow wounded him, and he returned to France for treatment. In 1612, Champlain was named lieutenant governor of New France. In 1613, he received funding for another voyage to New France. He explored the Ottawa River before returning to France. Two years passed before Champlain returned to New France.

Champlain took four Catholic Church missionaries on the 1615 expedition to New France. He hoped to convert the Native Peoples to Christianity. During this expedition, Champlain travelled on foot and by canoe through

■ This hand-coloured woodcut shows Champlain helping the Algonquin and Montagnais defeat the Iroquois at Lake Champlain in 1609. In return, the Algonquin and Montagnais provided pelts for the fur trade and guided Champlain on his expeditions through New France.

Champlain's Second Voyage 1615

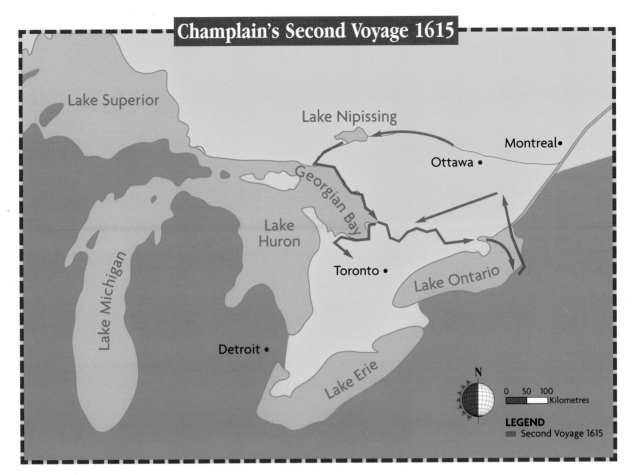

Lake Superior

Lake Nipissing

Montreal•

Ottawa •

Georgian Bay

Lake Huron

Lake Michigan

Toronto •

Lake Ontario

Detroit •

Lake Erie

N

0 50 100
Kilometres

LEGEND
Second Voyage 1615

the area between Georgian Bay and Lake Ontario. With the aid of the Huron, he ventured through Allumettes Island, the Mattawa River, Lake Nipissing, and the French River before reaching Lake Huron. Champlain and the Huron crossed Lake Ontario, arriving at an Iroquois village, where they attacked the Iroquois. Champlain was wounded. While recovering, Champlain created detailed accounts of the Huron culture and way of life. Soon after, he returned to France.

Between 1616 and 1620, Champlain briefly visited New France each year. He remained in New France for the summer before returning to France. He did not continue to explore the land.

Explorer Essentials

In 1611, Champlain married Hélène Boullé, a wealthy 12-year-old girl. Her wealth helped fund his expeditions.

Strengthening a Colony

When Champlain travelled to New France in 1620, he brought his young wife along. Hélène remained in New France for 4 years. During this time, Quebec's population grew as more settlers travelled from Europe. The settlers relied on food supplies from France. In 1626, France entered a war with Great Britain. By 1628, British ships prevented the French from carrying supplies along the St. Lawrence River to settlers.

In 1629, a fleet of British ships arrived in Quebec. By this time, the settlers were starving, forcing them to surrender. Champlain was taken to England as a prisoner until 1632. The 1632 Treaty of St. Germain-en-Laye restored France's control of New France. France renamed Champlain lieutenant governor, and he returned to New France in 1633. Champlain died of a **stroke** on December 25, 1635, in Quebec.

■ Hélène Boullé often taught Huron children in the Quebec settlement. After Champlain's death, Hélène became a nun.

Laurentian Mountains

Lac Saint Jean

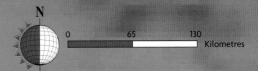

N

0   65   130
Kilometres

QUEBEC

St. Maurice River

St. Lawrence River

Appalachian Mountains

Explorer Essentials

Champlain left a collection of written works that was later published in six volumes. He also documented the first accurate maps of New France. For his work charting the New World, Champlain was dubbed the "Father of New France."

Suffering at Sea and on Land

While at sea and in New France, Champlain and his crew endured many hardships. From disease to wounds, many crewmembers suffered. Others had to work very hard to make up for the lack of participation of sick and injured crewmembers. On nearly every journey Champlain took to New France, some crewmembers died from scurvy. Others were not prepared for the bitter climate and fell ill during the harsh winters. Some of Champlain's companions received war wounds after being caught in the crossfire of rival Native Peoples.

Explorer Essentials

Champlain was the first European to settle in Port Royal. For thousands of years before Champlain's arrival, two Algonquian-speaking Native groups, the Mi'kmaq and Abenaki, already lived there.

Champlain faced great hardships during his first winter in New France. While living on an island in the St. Croix River, Champlain and his crew found the winter weather intolerable. As well, the location was unsatisfactory. Champlain settled on the island because he believed it would be easier to defend from potential attackers. However, the icy terrain and deep snow made it difficult for the

■ Champlain recognized the need to use Native Peoples' methods of transportation, and their knowledge and assistance at navigating New France's land.

settlers to search for food or water. Nearly the entire crew died, and of those who lived, only a few remained in New France.

The next winter, in 1605, the crew settled in Port Royal. To cope with ongoing misfortune, Champlain developed the L'Ordre de Bon Temps, or the Order of Good Cheer. According to the Order, crewmembers took turns creating robust meals for each other. They prepared fresh fish and game for all members of the crew. There was also entertainment and fun in the form of plays and dancing. By eating and having fun, the crew remained healthier.

■ Champlain created the Order of Good Cheer to lift his crew's spirits during the harsh Port Royal winter.

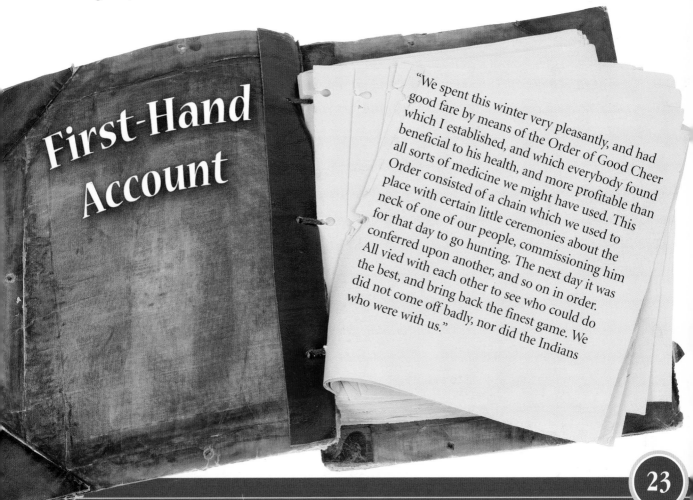

First-Hand Account

"We spent this winter very pleasantly, and had good fare by means of the Order of Good Cheer which I established, and which everybody found beneficial to his health, and more profitable than all sorts of medicine we might have used. This Order consisted of a chain which we used to place with certain little ceremonies about the neck of one of our people, commissioning him for that day to go hunting. The next day it was conferred upon another, and so on in order. All vied with each other to see who could do the best, and bring back the finest game. We did not come off badly, nor did the Indians who were with us."

Lasting Achievements and Legacies

Champlain enjoyed a long career as one of the world's most influential explorers. Mapping New France, establishing a healthy relationship with the Native Peoples, and building a colony are just a few of Champlain's achievements.

Champlain worked with the Huron, Montagnais, and Algonquin Native Peoples, and visited areas that were previously uncharted by European explorers. Champlain based his maps on information he acquired while exploring. He interviewed Native Peoples and used mathematical calculations. In 1609, Champlain fought alongside these groups in a war against the Iroquois. This started a feud between the Iroquois and the French that lasted more than 90 years.

Champlain ensured that control of the fur trade at the colony of Quebec was well protected. The site was built where the St. Lawrence River narrows. In 1627, Cardinal Richelieu, who worked for the king of France, created the Company of One Hundred Associates. Under the company, new fur trade settlements were built at Trois-Rivières in 1634, and Montreal in 1642.

■ Champlain paved the way for future settlements on New France's land. Before fertile land was farmed, settlers cleared the area of trees.

Champlain's legacy lives on today in the historic sites and landmarks named in his honour.

In 1609, Champlain became the first European to discover the lake that now bears his name while travelling with the Montagnais. Lake Champlain runs along the Missisquois Bay and the Richelieu River in Québec, emptying into the St. Lawrence. The lake creates a natural border between New York and Vermont. It has been the site of many battles between warring Native Peoples, as well as the War of 1812, the Seven Years War, and the Revolutionary War. Today, Lake Champlain is a busy commercial seaway. Many communities are built along Lake Champlain.

The Lake Champlain Maritime Museum shares Champlain's name. The museum hosts numerous exhibits and learning experiences, including shipwrecks, artifacts, **replicas**, and live demonstrations.

The Lake Champlain Underwater Historic Preserve System aims to preserve shipwrecks for public viewing and historical research. The system protects several wrecks from damage by anchoring boats and debris.

■ A statue of Champlain was built to celebrate the 300th anniversary of his second voyage up the Ottawa River in 1615. Sculptor Hamilton MacCarthy accidentally created the statue with Champlain holding his astrolabe upside down.

Explorer Expeditions

Many explorers voyaged to Canada in search of riches and new lands to claim for European merchants.

John Cabot

John Cabot was an explorer and navigator for Great Britain, although he was born in Italy. Cabot tried to find the Northwest Passage. He was not successful. Cabot was the first to claim the country of Canada as a British territory.

← Cabot 1497

Jacques Cartier

Jacques Cartier was a French explorer who looked for the Northwest Passage. He led three trips to Canada trying to find a route through North America to Asia. Cartier was responsible for naming Canada, from the Huron-Iroquois term *Kanata*.

← Cartier 1534
← Cartier 1535 & 1541

Samuel de Champlain

Samuel de Champlain was a French explorer and navigator. Champlain mapped much of the northeast portion of North America. As well, he established a settlement in Quebec. Champlain played an important role in running the colony of Quebec in the New World.

← Champlain 1603
← Champlain 1615

Henry Hudson

Henry Hudson was a British explorer and navigator. He explored the northeast portion of North America and parts of the Arctic Ocean. Hudson tried to find the Northwest Passage by searching south of Canada, in the United States.

← Hudson 1609
← Hudson 1610

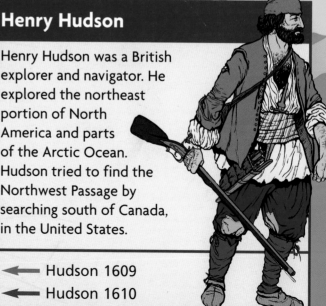

Hudson Bay

James Bay

CANADA

Strait of Belle Isle

LABRADOR

NEWFOUNDLAND

Anticosti Island

Gaspé Peninsula

Gulf of St. Lawrence

CAPE BRETON

PRINCE EDWARD ISLAND

Stadacona (Quebec)

Hochelaga (Montreal)

St. Lawrence River

NOVA SCOTIA

Atlantic Ocean

Lake Nipissing

Georgian Bay

Lake Ontario

N

0   115   230
Kilometres

27

Time Line

1567 Samuel de Champlain is born to Antoine Champlain and Marguerite Le Roy in Brouage, France.

1562–1598 The Wars of Religion take place between the Huguenots and the Catholics in France. Champlain serves as a quartermaster in the French army.

1599 Champlain acts as captain aboard his uncle's ship, the *St. Julien*. He sails to the West Indies, charting his observations.

1601 Champlain receives a large property near LaRochelle from his uncle. He also receives a small pension for his service as a geographer to King Henry IV.

1603 Champlain sails on his first voyage between France and New France. The boat docks at Tadoussac. Champlain sails up the St. Lawrence River and the Saguenay River to the St. Louis rapids. He also sails up to Gaspé.

1604 Champlain returns to New France. With his crew, he settles on an island in the St. Croix River. They later relocate to Port Royal.

1608 Champlain establishes the first permanent European colony in New France. It is named Quebec.

1609 Champlain fights with Huron, Algonquin, and Montagnais in wars against the Iroquois.

1610 During a brief visit to New France, Champlain is wounded by an arrow in a fight with the Iroquois. He returns to France for treatment.

1611 Champlain weds Hélène Boullé, a wealthy 12-year-old girl. Her wealth helps fund his expeditions.

1612 Champlain is named the lieutenant governor of New France.

1613 Champlain explores the Ottawa River.

1615 Champlain brings four missionaries of the Catholic Church on the expedition to New France. He travels through the area between Georgian Bay and Lake Ontario, Allumettes Island, the Mattawa River, Lake Nipissing, and the French River before reaching Lake Huron. This is his last exploration of the land.

1616–1620 Champlain makes brief visits each year to New France.

1620 Hélène Boullé travels to New France with Champlain. She remains for 4 years before returning to France.

1626 France enters a war with Great Britain.

1628 British ships cut off supplies to the French settlers living along the St. Lawrence River.

1629 Champlain is taken to England as a prisoner until 1632.

1633 France renames Champlain lieutenant governor, and he returns to New France.

1635 Champlain dies of a stroke in Quebec.

Create a Compass

Explorers, such as Champlain, often used a compass to guide them on their journeys. You can make your own compass.

Materials
Paper clip
Magnet
Packing foam
Bowl
Water

Instructions

1. Straighten the paper clip.
2. Rub the magnet along the straightened paper clip.
3. Break off a small piece of packing foam. Stick one end of the paper clip into the foam chip.
4. Fill the bowl with water. Place the paper clip and foam into the water.
5. The paper clip will rotate until it is pointing in the direction of the magnetic North Pole.

Quiz

1. When was Champlain's first voyage as captain? What was the name of his ship? Where did he travel?

2. When did Champlain first travel to New France?

3. When did Champlain establish the first permanent European colony? What is the name of the colony? Where was this colony located?

4. Why was Champlain sent to New France?

5. Which Native Peoples did Champlain encounter in New France?

6. What did Champlain create to pass the long winter nights?

7. When was Champlain's last voyage of exploration?

8. What happened to Champlain in 1629?

9. What is the name of the company established by Cardinal Richelieu? When was it created? What was its purpose?

10. When did Champlain die?

Answers

1. 1599, St. Julien, West Indies
2. 1603
3. 1608, Quebec, along the St. Lawrence River
4. to establish control of the fur trade for France
5. the Algonquin, Huron, Montagnais, and Iroquois
6. the Order of Good Cheer
7. 1615
8. He was taken prisoner by England until 1632.
9. the Company of One Hundred Associates, 1627, to populate New France
10. December 25, 1635

Web Sites

To learn more fascinating facts about Champlain, visit:
A Virtual Education Project, Virtualology.com
www.samueldechamplain.com

To learn more about explorers and Champlain, visit:
Virtual Museum of New France, The Explorers
www.civilization.ca/vmnf/explor/champ_e1.html

For information about explorers, visit:
Library and Archives Canada, Passageways
www.collectionscanada.ca/explorers/kids/h3-1410-e.html

Books

Faber, Harold. *Samuel de Champlain, Explorer of Canada*. New York:
Benchmark Books, 2004.

Sonneborn, Liz. *Samuel de Champlain*. New York: Franklin Watts, 2001.

Glossary

boatswain the person responsible for a ship's anchors, cables, and deck crew

cartographer someone who makes maps or charts

civil rights the freedoms and privileges belonging to a person living in a certain place

colonial a group of people from a distant country who form a settlement, but remain under the rule of another country

colony a community of people who have settled in a new area

latitude the distance measured north or south from the equator

magnetic field a field of force that is generated by electric currents

mariner a sailor

massacres cruel killings of large numbers of people or animals

masts tall posts that hold up a ship's sails

merchants people who buy and sell goods

monopolies total control by one group to produce or sell a certain item

navigator the person who plans which direction a ship will travel

parson a church leader

quartermaster an officer responsible for troops' food, clothing, and equipment

replicas copies

rigging the ropes and chains on a ship that support and work the sails

stroke loss of brain function owing to a broken blood vessel in the brain

ventilation allow fresh air to flow and replace stale air

weevils beetles

Index